T0344554

Some Aspects of the Labour
History of Bengal in the
Nineteenth Century

Other Titles in the Series

Social Science across Disciplines is a new series that brings to a general audience a selection from the papers and lectures delivered at the Centre for Studies in Social Sciences, Calcutta (CSSSC), over the last four decades. They fall into two categories—first, a selection from among the Occasional Papers circulated by the Centre's faculty, and second, from the two series of memorial lectures in the name of Sakharam Ganesh Deuskar (for lectures on Indian History and Culture) and of Romesh Chunder Dutt (for lectures on Political Economy).

Dipesh Chakrabarty
Ranajit Das Gupta

Some Aspects of the Labour History of Bengal in the Nineteenth Century

Two Views

Introduction by
Janaki Nair

Centre for Studies
in Social Sciences, Calcutta

OXFORD
UNIVERSITY PRESS

OXFORD
UNIVERSITY PRESS

Oxford University Press is a department of the University of Oxford.
It furthers the University's objective of excellence in research, scholarship,
and education by publishing worldwide. Oxford is a registered trademark of
Oxford University Press in the UK and in certain other countries.

Published in India by
Oxford University Press
2/11 Ground Floor, Ansari Road, Daryaganj, New Delhi 110 002, India

ISBN-13 (print edition): 978-0-19-948667-0
ISBN-10 (print edition): 0-19-948667-0

ISBN-13 (eBook): 978-0-19-909563-6
ISBN-10 (eBook): 0-19-909563-9

Typeset in Berling LT Std 10/14
by Tranistics Data Technologies, Kolkata 700 091
Printed in India by Replika Press Pvt. Ltd

Contents

About the Authors

Dipesh Chakrabarty studied Physics at Presidency College, Calcutta, and Management at the Indian Institute of Management Calcutta. He received a PhD in History from Australian National University, Canberra. After having taught for several years at the University of Melbourne, he is now the Lawrence A. Klimpton Distinguished Service Professor of History and South Asian Languages and Literature at the University of Chicago. He has held visiting appointments at several institutions around the world. He is the author of *Rethinking Working Class History: Bengal 1890–1940* (1989), *Provincializing Europe: Postcolonial Thought and Historical Difference* (2000), *Habitations of Modernity* (2002), and *The Calling of History: Sir Jadunath Sarkar and his Empire of Truth* (2015). He has also published two volumes of essays in Bengali. The paper reprinted in this volume was written when he was a fellow in History at the CSSSC from 1974 to mid-1976.

Ranajit Das Gupta studied Economics at the University of Calcutta. In his youth, he was closely involved with the labour movement and the Communist Party of India. After teaching for several years at Ananda Mohan College, Calcutta, he was a Fellow at CSSSC in the 1970s, before joining the Indian Institute of Management Calcutta, as a member of its faculty. His books include *Problems of Economic Transition: Indian Case Study* (1970), *Economy, Society and Politics in Bengal: Jalpaiguri 1869–1947* (1992), and *Labour and Working Class in Eastern India* (1994).

About the Editors

Partha Chatterjee is Professor of Anthropology and of Middle Eastern, South Asian and African Studies at Columbia University, New York, USA. A member of the CSSSC faculty for 36 years, he was also its Director from 1997 to 2007, and continues as Honorary Professor of Political Science. Among his books are *Nationalist Thought and the Colonial World* (1986), *The Nation and Its Fragments: Colonial and Postcolonial Histories* (1993), *A Princely Impostor? The Strange and Universal History of the Kumar of Bhawal* (2001), *The Politics of the Governed* (2004), and *The Black Hole of Empire* (2012).

Rosinka Chaudhuri is Director and Professor of Cultural Studies at the CSSSC. She is also the first Mellon Professor of the Global South at the University of Oxford. She has written *Gentlemen Poets in Colonial Bengal* (2002), *Freedom and Beef Steaks* (2012), and

The Literary Thing (2013) and edited *Derozio, Poet of India* (2008), *The Indian Postcolonial* (co-edited, 2010), *A History of Indian Poetry in English* (2016), and *An Acre of Green Grass and Other English Writings of Buddhadeva Bose* (2018). She has also translated and introduced *Rabindranath Tagore: Letters from a Young Poet* (2014).

About the Introduction Writer

Janaki Nair has been teaching History at the Centre for Historical Studies, Jawaharlal Nehru University, New Delhi, since 2009, before which she was at the CSSSC between 2002 and 2009. Beginning with an interest in labour history, she has also written on the history of law, urban history, and visual culture. In addition, she has a research interest in feminism and women's history. Her books include *Miners and Millhands: Work, Culture and Politics in Princely Mysore* (1998); *The Promise of the Metropolis: Bangalore's Twentieth Century* (2005; for which she won the New India Book Prize) and *Mysore Modern: Rethinking the Region under Princely Rule* (2011). She has also produced a film based on her labour history of Kolar Gold Field, entitled *After the Gold* (1997). She is a founding member of the Association of Indian Labour Historians.

General Introduction to the Series

Partha Chatterjee and *Rosinka Chaudhuri*

This series of publications from Oxford University Press brings to a general audience a selection of the papers and lectures delivered at the Centre for Studies in Social Sciences, Calcutta (CSSSC), over the last four decades. They fall into two categories: first, a chosen few from among the Occasional Papers circulated by the Centre's faculty and second, from the two series of memorial lectures in the name of Sakharam Ganesh Deuskar, for lectures on Indian history and culture, and Romesh Chunder Dutt, for lectures on political economy.

The CSSSC was founded in 1973 as an autonomous research institute financed primarily by the Indian Council for Social Science Research and the Government of West Bengal. Since then, the Centre, as it is ubiquitously known, has established an academic reputation that places it at the crest of research institutes of excellence in India. Its faculty works in the fields of history, political science, sociology, social anthropology, geography, economics, and cultural studies. Its unique interdisciplinary culture allows for collaborations between scholars from different fields of research that might not find support in traditional department-based institutions, attracting students and researchers from across the country and abroad.

The R.C. Dutt Lectures at the CSSSC have focused on themes from economic theory, economic history, and development policy, mostly relating to India. As is well known, Romesh Chunder Dutt (1848–1909) served in the Indian Civil Service from 1871 to 1897. On retirement, he lectured at the University of London, UK, and wrote his classic work in two volumes, *The Economic History of India under Early British Rule* (1902) and *The Economic History of India in the Victorian Age* (1904). He was elected president of the 1899 session of the Indian National Congress. Apart from his extensive writings on the colonial economy, the condition of the peasantry, famines, and land rights, Dutt was also a poet in English and a novelist in Bengali, writing on historical and social themes. Over the years, some of the most eminent economists of India have delivered the R.C. Dutt lectures at the Centre. Among them are Sukhamoy Chakrabarti, K.N. Raj, V.M. Dandekar, Ashok Rudra, Krishna Bharadwaj, A. Vaidyanathan, Suresh Tendulkar, Prabhat Patnaik, I.S. Gulati, Amit Bhaduri, C.T. Kurien, Praveen Visaria, Kaushik Basu, Geeta Sen, Debraj Ray, Abhijit V. Banerjee, Ravi Kanbur, and Dilip Mookerjee. The lectures selected for publication in the present series will capture key debates among Indian economists in the last four decades in topics such as the crisis of planning, economic liberalization, inequality, gender and development, sustainable growth, and the effects of globalization.

The S.G. Deuskar Lectures began as a series on Indian nationalism but widened to reflect the cross-disciplinary interests the CSSSC nurtured, featuring a range of distinguished speakers on the history, culture, politics, and society of India. Sakharam Ganesh Deuskar (1869–1912) was Maharashtrian by ancestry and member of a family that migrated in the mid-eighteenth century to the Santal Parganas on the border of Bihar and Bengal. A schoolteacher and journalist by profession, he is best known for his Bengali tract *Desher Katha* (1904)—a damning indictment of the exploitative and violent character of British colonial rule—which is reported to have sold 13,000 copies in five editions within five years during the Swadeshi movement in Bengal. Some of the finest scholars and artists of modern India have delivered the Deuskar Lectures, including, among historians, Ranajit Guha, Tapan Raychaudhuri, Irfan Habib, Satish Chandra, Romila Thapar, Partha Sarathi Gupta, Sabyasachi Bhattacharya, Sumit Sarkar, Dipesh Chakrabarty, Muzaffar Alam, Gyanendra Pandey, Sanjay Subrahmanyam, and Shahid Amin; among philosophers, J.N. Mohanty and Bimal Krishna Matilal; among artists and art critics, Geeta Kapur, Vivan Sundaram, K.G. Subramanyan, and Ghulam Mohammed Sheikh; among social theorists, Gayatri Chakravorty Spivak, Sudipta Kaviraj, and Veena Das. A selection of these lectures will now be reprinted in this current initiative from Oxford University Press.

Occasional Papers published by the CSSSC represent the research of the CSSSC faculty over the years. Many of these papers were later published in journals and books, some becoming classic essays that are essential reading for students and researchers in the field. Some of the most important works in the Indian social sciences, it would be fair to say, are represented here in the form of papers or drafts of book chapters. Of the nearly 200 Occasional Papers published so far, we will reprint in the present series only those that are not already in wide circulation as journal articles or book chapters. Included among our Occasional Papers will be the current initiative of the Archives Series Occasional Papers, meant specifically to showcase the collection in the CSSSC visual archives.

By turning these outstanding papers into little books that stand on their own, our series is not intended as a survey of disciplinary fields. Rather, the intention is to present to the reader within a concise format an intellectual encounter with some of the foremost practitioners in the field of humanities and social sciences in India. R.K. Narayan, in his childhood memoir, *My Days* (1947), had written that when, as young men, he and his friends had discussed starting a journal and were thinking of names for it, someone suggested 'Indian Thought'. 'There is no such thing' was the witty response from a friend. Narayan nevertheless began publishing *Indian Thought*, a quarterly of literature, philosophy, and culture, which lasted all of one year. We suggest that this series might, in the end, prove his friend wrong.

Preface

It is a mixed privilege to have something of one's eristic youth brought into the glare of public attention decades later. Mixed, because from so far away in time, I can only look at the sharp edges of my polemical prose with a remote sense of amusement; and yet it is undeniable that the issues debated here were of capital importance in the early phase of my development as a historian. But personal history apart, what this debate testifies to is the importance attached to the question of consciousness in certain Marxist circles of Calcutta in the 1960s and 1970s. The criticism I received in the 1990s for the perceived 'culturalism' of these exchanges or for my untimely use of the adjective 'primordial'— once a respectable word now fallen into disrepute—in qualifying human relationships to caste or religion, often missed the context that made questions of working-class culture truly controversial. 'Consciousness' assumed a theoretical importance because it was thought that a 'working class' born in the deprived conditions of a colony could not depend merely on 'objective' circumstances for the development of a class-outlook, so indispensable for the overthrow of capitalist relations. Understanding workers' culture and raising consciousness would have to be the first task of any revolutionary project. Right or wrong, that was the debate.

Sadly, Ranajit Dasgupta, my interlocutor, is no longer with us. My appreciation of his work may be found in what I wrote in his memory in *Economic and Political Weekly*, 33 (38), 19 September 1998.

Dipesh Chakrabarty
Chicago, 25 August 2018

Introduction

'Class Consciousness': A Concept in Crisis or in Terminal Decline?

Janaki Nair

A spectre—of a post-work world where 'humans need not apply'[1]—is increasingly haunting the imaginations, and more importantly, driving the research agendas of those who are sizing up the scale of a change that will be like no other that has gone before it. The predicaments and possible futures of the 'precariat' that has replaced the secure, committed, spatially rooted working class are a concern more of sociologists, economists, and political scientists than, naturally, historians. But even among historians, the 'proletariat'— endowed with the world historical role of transforming capitalism itself—now appears like a museumized fossil, a chimera of the past that holds no more than nostalgic value. With the rise of information-rich technologies and forms of immaterial labour, greater uncertainty regarding the relevance of skills, greater informality, and greater inequality are the features of the workplace. The end of 'work' as we once knew it has important consequences not only for modes of political mobilization in the present, but also for the study and analysis of our pasts. What life, therefore, does a debate on class consciousness between two scholars more than three decades ago have among historians of the subcontinent in general, and labour and working-class historians in particular?

The brief, and sharply posed, exchange between Dipesh Chakrabarty and Ranajit Das Gupta, entitled 'Some Aspects of the Labour History of Bengal in the Nineteenth Century: Two Views'[2] was sparked off by two previous Occasional Papers, 11 and 22, authored by Chakrabarty and Das Gupta, respectively.[3] The exchange, and the articles they were based on, revealed at least three levels of difference between the authors, which continue to have some resonance for our times: theoretical/conceptual, political/ethical, and methodological.

The chosen theoretical orientation of each author's investigations into working-class consciousness in the same region, period, and industry marks the first difference. Which labour historian has not been mesmerized by E.P. Thompson's magisterial work, *The Making of the English Working Class?*[4] Both authors here are clearly under his spell. At the end of nearly 900 pages, Thompson had convinced readers that consciousness is not a mechanical outcome of the capitalist mode of production, not a thing but a process; that even failure must be taken on board in order to flesh out that process; that not only was the working class present (and therefore conscious) of its own making, but drew from rich pre-capitalist cultural traditions of dissent, rebellion, and republicanism.

Nowhere in his book did Thompson feel compelled to specify the Marxist theorist who animated his work, allowing instead the captivating narrative to tell its tale. It speaks, perhaps, of a subcontinental preoccupation that the preferred Marxist framework is spelled out here with such obvious relish by each author. Therefore, arguably the most important of the differences that were investigated in these two articles was what indeed accounted not just for the 'low-classness' of workers (the term used by Sabyasachi Bhattacharya to describe the pervasive surrogation phenomena of the

middle-class representation of labour in India[5])
but for the unprecedented and disruptive
Talla riot of 1897.[6] Participation in this riot by
relatively fresh Muslim immigrants from the
North-West Provinces and Bihar, who readily
rallied to the pan-Islamic call, produced not a
little discomfort among labour historians. Was
the allegiance to religion (or other non-class
identity such as language, caste, or ethnicity)
merely transitional in an incompletely capitalist
(because colonial) economy? Would it decline
or disappear as working-class experience of
factory work deepened and when alternative
organizational forms became available? Or
were affiliations to religion, region, caste,
and language more than just residues of
peasant consciousness, a 'primordial loyalty'
(Chakrabarty's preferred term[7]) that was
irreducibly stable and long-lived, defining ways
of being in the new urban location?

An approach to answering these questions
lay in the two other differences between
the two historians. While both historians
therefore relied largely on similar official
sources in their construction of working-
class history, and both revealed their debt to
the rich and complex heritage of Marxism,
their interpretations were founded on the

possibility, or not, of emerging working-class consciousness. Ranajit Das Gupta was an activist, with a background in peasant and working-class organizing. His rich empirical research on working-class life and protest in the colonial period made links with contemporary forms of protest, and the visionary futures of the Communist Party of India. In this, he was part of a long (and one must admit, until recently, hardy) historical tradition, which analysed non-class identities as needless distractions—no, 'deviations'[8]—on the road to class consciousness.[9] Chakrabarty faulted Das Gupta for falling prey to this impulse, and instead privileged a methodological focus on the community consciousness of the migrant to explain the Talla riot of 1897. On the one hand was the unreconstructed Third Internationalist Marxism of Ranajit Das Gupta; on the other, Dipesh Chakrabarty's reliance on the anti-vanguardist Antonio Gramsci.

The political or moral charge which was so evident in Ranajit Das Gupta's reading of the same material defined his economistic methodological focus as well. He relied on wages, hours, and conditions of work and the material miseries of the nascent working class.

These early experiences, and not the residues of a peasant life, determined their actions and lives: workers were 'mere cogs on a complex mechanism';[10] they were 'characterised by a good many ethnic, religious, caste and other differences' but common interest and solidarity was 'beginning to get an upper hold on the workers' minds….'[11] The demand for a holiday for Bakr-Eid or Muharram, rather than a few hours off work, was no more than a veiled class demand for reduced working hours and more leisure.[12]

If there was discrimination between Muslim and Hindu workers, it was part of the management's artful ploy to 'foster fissiparous tendencies among workers….'[13] Since all, and not just Muslim workers, suffered from the exploitation in the mills, their reactions cannot be explained in 'narrow sectarian terms'.[14] In the absence, says Das Gupta, 'of any alternative ideology and programme, the country people, now in the process of becoming factory workers, were compelled to turn towards traditional customs and religion'.[15] The teleology that Chakrabarty found fault with was embarrassingly evident.

On the contrary, Chakrabarty argued from a culturalist perspective: in order to take

E.P. Thompson's problematic, and not only his rhetoric, seriously, one would have to acknowledge that the cultural inheritance of the Indian worker bore little resemblance to that of the English worker. This inheritance was divisive, hierarchical, and even when religious, contained no seeds of redemptive Methodism or radical non-conformism, with its promise of equality and justice.

Indeed, one could argue that both authors, lacking the embarrassment of riches that British social historians had used so creatively, brought their speculative historical imaginations to bear on conventional material that was suggestive at best. Chakrabarty admitted that 'much of what I say is conjectural'.[16] Predictably, a good part of his construction of community consciousness (as opposed to communal consciousness, which he usefully distinguishes between) is derived by inference. 'Undoubtedly', the sardar in his capacity as recruiter 'would have become extremely important to the worker'.[17] 'Perhaps' the Bengali bhadralok leader felt distant from 'the world of men who worked in the mills' and possibly, 'community consciousness' was 'the migrant workers' substitute for closed shop communalism'.[18]

More important, in this lively exchange, was the charge of 'ahistoricity' that was made by both authors.[19] Both authors agreed on the stifling effects of colonialism on the economic transformation of the subcontinent. But to Chakrabarty, Das Gupta had stuck so closely to the English template as to miss both the peculiarities of the English, and the specificities of the Indian setting. Das Gupta, in turn, averred that the exclusive focus on 'community consciousness' had blinded Chakrabarty to the other collective actions and solidarities of workers.[20]

In this exchange, and judging from the somewhat petulant though resolutely economistic response of Das Gupta, Chakrabarty won the day. The latter had raised a question that was to be a particular burden of all subcontinental labour historians: What are the aspects of working-class lives that cannot be explained by, or subsumed under, the capital-labour conflict? Why was labour militancy too often accompanied by persistent organizational weakness? And why were all collective public actions of workers marked by an inherent duality, which often dissolved class solidarities into fights between workers themselves, on religious or ethnic lines, spectacularly as in Bombay in 1893 and 1929?[21]

Interestingly, Chakrabarty's Achilles' heel turned out to be his insistence on the 'actual empirical consciousness' of the worker,[22] on 'what actually goes on in people's minds in specific historical junctures'[23] or for that matter within people's heads.[24] Chakrabarty had no more privileged access to this than Das Gupta, certainly no more than what a creative historical imagination would permit. It was no surprise then that the most important challenges to Chakrabarty's confident, if thought-provoking, assertions were labour historians working on other industries, cities, and regions, for whom his arguments about a 'primordial loyalty' were empirically unfounded and conceptually flawed since they were profoundly 'ahistorical'. Rajnarayan Chandavarkar, perhaps the most severe of Chakrabarty's critics, remarked that the worker's cultural inheritance in the latter's hands had 'turned into a static, timeless, indeed Orientalist characterisation of a "traditional" Indian—implicitly "Hindu" culture—in Bengal, a predominantly Muslim province'.[25] No inheritance, as Chandavarkar decisively demonstrated in his own thick and innovative description of Girangaon in Bombay in the early twentieth century, was impervious to the new cleavages and solidarities that were enabled, as much on the shop floor as in the neighbourhoods. The 'neighbourhoods were not therefore, the repositories of the primordial loyalties of the working class'.[26] That Chandavarkar himself proposed that working-class actions, no matter how contradictory, were a *rational* response to material conditions, did not undermine the pioneering quality of his work on non-workplace concerns and the duplex role of neighbourhood affiliations.[27]

Broadly, the close investigation of new ties that were forged in the city, new family strategies, and the altered scale of kin and regional networks in the cities of Bombay and Kanpur was enabled in the work of other historians like Radha Kumar and Chitra Joshi. They painted a far more nuanced, contingent, and yet refreshing portrait of a working class in the making, which was both methodologically and conceptually innovative.[28] These works, and many others that emerged in the 1990s and early 2000s, were at a remove from the stultifying frames that either posited eternally rebellious workers, or workers mired in their ascribed identities. Historians were now encouraged to acknowledge the creative use of religious symbols that were made by union organizers, even left-wing ones.[29] Others brought in the contradictory opportunities offered by capitalism to women,[30] those of the oppressed castes less often,[31] tribes, generating new perspectives that benefitted both labour history and social history more generally.[32]

There were early signs that the search for radical artisanal traditions could overlook other desires and longings of workers.[33] But in the new millennium, many obituaries of the 'working class' have been written (for which the *International Labour and Working Class History* journal provided a hospitable home[34]). As a political subject, on whom many revolutionary hopes were mistakenly pinned; as a unified economic category, whose foundational exclusions were exposed; as a site of a more ambiguous 'consciousness' than class alone—a fatal preoccupation with working-class consciousness may have led to a certain blindness.[35] Such notices were met with fierce, and sometimes, one must admit, moralistic, reassertions in India and elsewhere, of the continued importance of class as an analytical category, and as a political force.

Obituaries to class have been far fewer in India, but there is no doubt a discernible shift, and narrowing interest in questions of class consciousness, whether in the political or academic domain. Some proxy discussions of class consciousness have nevertheless continued. Subho Basu's detailed 'revisit' of Bengal jute mill workers from the 1890s and his querying of the category of 'peasant worker' attempted to reconcile both the nuances proposed by Chakrabarty and the assertion of class solidarities by Das Gupta.[36] Parimal Ghosh has more appreciatively taken forward Chakrabarty's formulations, by making links between community and communal consciousness of the 1920s.[37] Arjan de Haan's anthropological approach to the history of migration to a jute mill area of Bengal provided some useful correctives to historians' certainties about the effects of capitalism or colonialism, and foregrounds migrants as rational, calculative strategists.[38] Other questions veered away from class consciousness towards structural aspects: the feminization of agricultural labour, for instance, or the constitutive role of gender in shaping the working class.[39]

This 'demise' of 'class consciousness' as a focus of interest has by no means diminished the importance of class as an analytical category, though its limits are today more readily recognized in labour history or in histories of work. The themes of the conferences, and extremely impressive output, of the Association of Indian Labour Historians, which has met every two years since 1995, are an indication of Indian labour history's new and very creative impulse. They have taken on questions that the excessive focus on the small but organized, factory-based working class had effectively overlooked. As Ravi Ahuja notes, there was an attention to labour in public life and the academy 'out of all proportion to the consistently small share of factory workers in India's workforce'.[40] How indeed, when there was/is a multiplicity of 'modes of production' dominated by non-factory, even non-urban work, could one place such emphasis on the urban, male, factory-based working class?

A powerful stimulus to labour history came from the currents of Indian feminism and caste politics, with extraordinary dividends. One might even say that Indian labour history got a fresh lease of life from these currents, as much as it was refreshed by other disciplinary orientations, notably that of anthropology.[41] A productive new strand of research, for instance, has been on the spectrum of free/unfree labour, on the vastly heterogeneous worlds of informal/unorganized labour,[42] ranging from domestic production and domestic care to sex work, from self-employed mechanics and fisherfolk to scavengers; indeed, labour history may well be recasting itself as a history of work more generally.[43]

Labour history, or a history of work, insofar as it is concerned with the lives of labour, in all its complexity, is also laying claim to the interests of a far larger body of social history. There is a danger of the distinction becoming blurred, of labour history vanishing into the far greater reaches of social and cultural history as the plebeian replaces the proletarian as the centre of this discourse. More recently, the 'history of everyday life' has proved to be a compelling attraction, turning away from the objective, structural, material institutional factors in labour history to the subjective, cultural, contingent, and more emotional aspects of working-class history.[44] Just as the disappointments about the failure of the nineteenth-century English working class to usher in a revolutionary political order absorbed British Marxists, or the regularity with which large-scale working-class struggles dissolved into communal or caste riots in the subcontinent furrowed the brows of Indian labour historians, the indisputable enthusiasm of the German workers for imperialism in 1914 and the working-class support of Hitler in 1933 called for explanation.

The turn to the quotidian, the affective, and the ephemeral may not replace the force and energy that was for so long enjoyed by the concept of the 'working class' and its contradictory consciousness. We may take heart in the fact that the (research) card-carrying historian will certainly go further in developing the more inclusive terms on which a new world may be thought.

Additional Reading

Joshi, Chitra. 'Histories of Indian Labour: Predicaments and Possibilities.' *History Compass* 6, no. 2 (2008): 439–54.

Kumar, Radha. 'Family and Factory: Women in the Bombay Cotton Textile Industry, 1919–1939.' *Indian Economic and Social History Review* 20, no. 1 (1983): 81–96.

Sarkar, Sumit. 'Review.' *Historical Materialism* 12, no. 3 (2004): 285–313.

Sen, Samita. 'Unsettling the Household: Act VI (of 1901) and the Regulation of Women Migrants in Colonial Bengal.' *International Review of Social History* 46, no. S4 (December 1996): 135–56.

van der Linden, Marcel. 'The "Globalization" of Labor and Working-Class History and Its Consequences.' *International Labor and Working-Class History*, no. 65, Agriculture and Working-Class Formation (Spring 2004): 136–56.

Notes and References

1. 'Humans Need Not Apply' is a portentous 15-minute video, factual, funny, and frightening in equal part, as it persuasively predicts the end of work and the redundancy of human labour as the 'bot' gains acceptance worldwide. See 'Humans Need Not Apply,' available at https://www.youtube.com/watch?v=7Pq-S557XQU.

2. Dipesh Chakrabarty and Ranajit Das Gupta, 'Some Aspects of the Labour History of Bengal in the Nineteenth Century: Two Views' (Occasional Paper 40, Centre for Studies in Social Sciences, Calcutta, October 1981).

3. Dipesh Chakrabarty, 'Communal Riots and Labour: Bengal's Jute Mill Hands in the 1890s' (Occasional Paper 11, Centre for Studies in Social Sciences, Calcutta, 1976); Ranajit Das Gupta, 'Material Conditions and Behavioural Aspects of Calcutta Working Class' (Occasional Paper 22, Centre for Studies in Social Sciences, Calcutta, 1978). I will, however, reference the published articles based on these Occasional Papers for easier access: Dipesh Chakrabarty,

'Communal Riots and Labour: Bengal's Jute Mill-Hands in the 1890s,' *Past & Present*, no. 91 (May 1981): 140–69; Ranajit Das Gupta, 'Poverty and Protest: A Study of Calcutta's Industrial Workers and Labouring Poor, 1875–1899', in *Labour and Working Class in Eastern India: Studies in Colonial History* (Calcutta: K.P. Bagchi and Co., 1994), 303–405.

4. E.P. Thompson, *The Making of the English Working Class* (1963; Harmondsworth: Penguin, 1968).

5. Sabyasachi Bhattacharya, 'Introduction', in 'Coolies, Capital and Colonialism: Studies in Indian Labour History', *International Review of Social History*, vol. 51, supplement 14 (2006): 7–8.

6. The Talla Riot refers to the riots that broke out in 1897 over the demolition of a purportedly illegal 'mosque' in north Calcutta; of the 87 people who were charged with rioting, 81 were convicted. The rioters included a large number of jute millhands.

7. Chakrabarty and Das Gupta, 'Some Aspects of Labour History of Bengal in the Nineteenth Century', 13.

8. K.N. Joglekar, who was working in the Girni Kamgar Mahadmandal in Bombay in 1923, had this to say: 'The workers were not quite class-conscious…. My task at this stage of the movement was to fight against these deviations and give a class attitude to the workers.' As cited in Sabyasachi Bhattacharya, 'The

Outsiders; A Historical Note', in *The Truth Unites: Essays in Honour of Samar Sen*, ed. Ashok Mitra (Calcutta: Subarnarekha, 1985), 94.

9. Chakrabarty cites the Bengali instances; see also, for instance, Thomas Isaac, 'From Caste Consciousness to Class Consciousness: Alleppey Coir Workers during Inter-War Period,' *Economic and Political Weekly*, vol. 20, no. 4 (26 January 1985): 5–18.

10. Das Gupta, 'Poverty and Protest', 315.

11. Das Gupta, 'Poverty and Protest', 329.

12. Chakrabarty and Das Gupta, 'Some Aspects of Labour History of Bengal in the Nineteenth Century', 31.

13. Das Gupta, 'Poverty and Protest', 348.

14. Das Gupta, 'Poverty and Protest', 349.

15. Das Gupta, 'Poverty and Protest', 380.

16. Chakrabarty, 'Communal Riots and Labour', 142.

17. Chakrabarty, 'Communal Riots and Labour', 153.

18. Chakrabarty, 'Communal Riots and Labour', 153.

19. Chakrabarty and Das Gupta, 'Some Aspects of Labour History of Bengal in the Nineteenth Century', 9, 27, 40.

20. Chakrabarty and Das Gupta, 'Some Aspects of Labour History of Bengal in the Nineteenth Century', 30.

21. Shashi Bhushan Upadhyay, 'Communalism and Working Class: Riot of 1893 in Bombay City', *Economic and Political Weekly*, vol. 24, no. 30 (29 July 1989): 69–75.

22. Chakrabarty and Das Gupta, 'Some Aspects of Labour History of Bengal in the Nineteenth Century', 14.

23. Chakrabarty and Das Gupta, 'Some Aspects of Labour History of Bengal in the Nineteenth Century', 16.

24. Chakrabarty and Das Gupta, 'Some Aspects of Labour History of Bengal in the Nineteenth Century', 17.

25. Rajnarayan Chandavarkar, '"The Making of the Working Class": E.P. Thompson and Indian History', *History Workshop Journal*, no. 43 (Spring 1997): 182.

26. Chandavarkar, '"The Making of the Working Class"', 184–5. See also Rajnarayan Chandavarkar, *The Origins of Industrial Capitalism in India: Business Strategies and the Working Classes in Bombay, 1900–1948* (Cambridge: Cambridge University Press, 1994), 168–238.

27. Explaining the disintegration of worker solidarity during strikes into communal riots, Chandavarkar said, 'Since workers often organized around ties of caste, kinship and village to secure jobs and to protect them, competition in the labour market *could* acquire a communal edge' (Chandavarkar, *The Origins of Industrial Capitalism in India*, 422 [emphasis added]).

28. Chitra Joshi, *Lost Worlds: Indian Labour and its Forgotten Histories* (Delhi: Permanent

Black, 2003). See also Radha Kumar, 'City Lives: Workers' Housing and Rent in Bombay, 1911–47', *Economic and Political Weekly*, vol. 22, no. 30 (25 July 1987): 47–56; Radha Kumar, 'Sex and Punishment among Mill-Workers in Early-twentieth Century Bombay', in *Changing Concepts of Rights in South Asia*, eds, Michael Anderson and Sumit Guha (New Delhi: Oxford University Press, 1998), 179–97.

29. Chandavarkar, *The Origins of Industrial Capitalism in India*, 213. See also Joshi, *Lost Worlds*, 282–3.

30. Samita Sen, *Women and Labour in Late Colonial India: The Bengal Jute Industry* (Cambridge: Cambridge University Press, 1999), 89–176. See also Kumar; Joshi, *Lost Worlds*.

31. Janaki Nair, *Miners and Millhands: Work, Culture and Politics in Princely Mysore* (Delhi: SAGE, 1998).

32. Dilip Simeon, *The Politics of Labour under Late Colonialism: Workers, Unions and the State in Chota Nagpur, 1928–1939* (Delhi: Manohar, 1995).

33. E.J. Hobsbawm and Joan Wallach Scott, 'Political Shoemakers', *Past & Present*, no. 89 (November 1980): 86–114. Jacques Rancière, 'The Myth of the Artisan: Critical Reflections on a Category of Social History', *International Labor and Working-Class History*, vol. 24 (Fall 1983): 1–16.

34. Joan W. Scott, 'The "Class" We Have Lost', *International Labor and Working-Class History*, vol. 57 (Spring 2000): 69–75.

35. Anupama Rao, 'Stigma and Labour: Remembering Dalit Marxism', *Seminar*, 2012, available at www.india-seminar.com/2012/633/633_anupama_rao.htm.

36. Subho Basu, *Does Class Matter? Colonial Capital and Workers' Resistance in Bengal (1890–1937)*, SOAS Studies on South Asia (Oxford: Oxford University Press, 2004).

37. Parimal Ghosh, 'Communalism and Colonial Labour: Experience of Calcutta Jute Mill Workers, 1880–1930', *Economic and Political Weekly*, vol. 25, no. 30 (28 July 1990): 61–72.

38. Arjan De Haan, *Unsettled Settlers: Migrant Workers and Industrial Capitalism in Calcutta*, (Hilversum: Verloren, 1994).

39. Shobhana Warrier, 'Condition of Women in Cotton Mills of Madras, Madurai and Coimbatore 1914–1939', *Social Scientist*, vol. 19, nos 5–6, May–June, 1991, pp. 42–59; Samita Sen '"Without His Consent?": Marriage and Women's Migration in Colonial India', *International Labor and Working-Class History*, no. 65, Agriculture and Working-Class Formation (Spring, 2004), pp. 77–104; Karuna Dietrich Wielenga, 'Repertoires of Resistance: The Handloom Weavers of South India, c. 1800–1960', *International Review of Social History*,

no. 61 (2016), pp. 423–58. More generally, see Chitra Joshi 'Histories of Indian Labour: Predicaments and Possibilities', *History Compass*, vol. 6, no. 2 (2008): 439–54.

40. Ravi Ahuja, ed., *Working Lives and Worker Militancy: The Political of Labour in Colonial India*, (New Delhi: Tulika Books, 2013), x.

41. Jonathan Parry, 'Lords of Labour: Working and Shirking in Bhilai,' *Contributions to Indian Sociology*, vol. 33, nos 1–2 (1999): 107–40.

42. P.P. Mohapatra, 'Regulated Informality: Legal Constructions of Labour Relations in Colonial India 1814–1926', in *Workers in the Informal Sector: Studies in Labour History 1800–2000*, eds, S. Bhattacharya and J. Lucassen (New Delhi: Macmillan, 2005).

43. Marcel van der Linden and Prabhu Mohapatra, eds, *Labour Matters: Towards Global Histories* (New Delhi: Tulika, 2009); Ahuja, *Working Lives and Worker Militancy*.

44. Alf Lüdtke, 'Cash Coffee, Horseplay: *Eigensinn* and Politics among Factory Workers in Germany circa 1900', in *Confrontation, Class Consciousness, and the Labour Process*, eds, Michael Hanagan and Charles Stephenson (New York: Praeger, 1986); Alf Lüdtke, 'People Working: Everyday Life and German Fascism', *History Workshop Journal*, no. 50 (Autumn 2000): 74–92.

Some Aspects of
the Labour History of
Bengal in the
Nineteenth Century

DIPESH CHAKRABARTY

RANAJIT DAS GUPTA

1. Class Consciousness and Labour History of Bengal: A Critique of Ranajit Das Gupta's Paper 'Material Conditions and Behavioural Aspects of Calcutta Working Class 1875–99'

Dipesh Chakrabarty*

> *It is only too often the case that the theory takes precedence over the historical material which it is intended to theorise. It is easy to suppose that class takes place, not as historical process, but inside our own heads. Of course we do not admit that it goes on only in our heads....*
>
> —E.P. Thompson, 1978[1]

Ranajit Das Gupta's paper contained important criticisms of my essay on 'Communal Riots and Labour' (CRL).[2] I am flattered by his attention and occasional complimentary references, but I do feel called upon to answer some of his charges and investigate our differences.[3] If the tone of my disagreement is sharp at places, it is not because I do not consider Das Gupta's work valuable. Even in opposing, one learns. But I am concerned about the ideas being put forward, and it is this sense of concern that my tone may betray.

The following are some of our differences that I have been able to pinpoint:

- Das Gupta finds my essay 'somewhat exaggerated' (p. 79).
- He finds my term 'community consciousness' 'too narrow' (p. 137).
- He implies (p. 150) that CRL in effect 'belittles' the 'significance' of the jute workers' struggles in the 1890s, when, according to him, the workers were showing '*class feeling*' (original emphasis) and were trying to become class conscious (p. 150).
- Das Gupta thus proposes 'class consciousness' against my 'community consciousness' as a better category for understanding the jute mill workers of the 1890s.

There are at least three specific instances where Das Gupta misreads the text of

CRL. His misreadings at times verge on misrepresentation.

- On p. 33, Das Gupta quotes from the Government of Bengal's reply to the Labour Commission of 1892, where the government denied the existence of any trade unions in Bengal and said that 'strikes and lockouts' played only 'a very small part' and that employer–employee relations 'have never been a cause of anxiety to Government'. He then says: 'One may pick out this passage to prove the absence of workers' open and direct action, and *sometimes this has been done*' (my emphasis). Who has done it? A footnote adds: 'Chakrabarty takes this position' in CRL, p. 7. And then follows a paragraph on how 'misleading' 'such a view' is, how it attaches 'undue importance' to things unimportant, and how, above all, it is *'factually erroneous'* (my emphasis) to conclude that the period before 1892 was one of working-class passivity.

I open CRL at p. 7 to discover that Chakrabarty does *not* take this position. In fact, the page in question is not about working-class reality, but about changes in government and capitalists' attitudes. I was arguing that even if labour gave no anxiety to the government and the IJMA before 1892, by 1895 it definitely did, and this could be a pointer to an intensification of labour unrest.

But this is not all. After stating on p. 33 how 'factually erroneous' it would be to see the pre-1892 period as one of lull, Das Gupta himself goes on to say on pp. 38–9:

> It must not be thought that battles of the early 1880s were immediately followed by further direct action of broader sweep and greater intensity. On the contrary, the period *from mid-1880s to mid-1890s was one of lull* [my emphasis]. In fact, up to 1893 there is no record of any open conflict between workers and their employers except [one] … [ii].

• Das Gupta (p. 139) takes me to task for suggesting that the formation in 1895 of a workers' association, which of its own choice gave itself the name Mahomedan Association, was indicative of the labourer's community consciousness. I wrote (CRL p. 36):

> It is only in this context [of sustained community consciousness] that we can understand why the first organisation of mill workers … would choose to call itself

Mahomedan Association, why it spent money on renovating mosques, and why it had as one of its principal aims recruitment of more Muslims to jute mill work. Community consciousness seems to have been the migrant worker's substitute for closed-shop trade unionism.

If anything, I would now criticize the last sentence as having been too economistic in spirit. But I don't see the point of Das Gupta's criticisms. He actually agrees that the association was more Muslim than anything else 'in its early days' (that is, about 1895), but then implies that, by 1908, things had turned, and on occasions, it held meetings to discuss working hours. 'Scarcely can one view all this as signs of merely communal outlook,' says Das Gupta, 'without any broader perspective of the working class ... trying to determine its labour-time and leisure' (p. 140).

Apart from pointing to the distinction that I make (see next) between 'community-consciousness' and 'communal outlook', let me also mention three other points here. First, my remarks were about the mid-1890s and not 1908. Second, going by Das Gupta's own material, the changes of 1908 do not seem to have been very profound. The association said (in 1908) that it was then trying 'to popularise mill work' (Das Gupta misses the importance of the significant word 'popularise') 'amongst the masses of the population in general and *Mussalmans in particular* [my emphasis]'. Why 'Mussalmans in particular'? This brings me to my third point. In 1905—and Das Gupta does not mention this—the association and its president were exhibiting distinctly pro-Muslim, pro-British, loyalist sentiments.[4] It would be difficult to explain all this purely in terms of labour-capital conflict.

• Das Gupta accuses (p. 127) me of arguing that the Talla riot of 1897 'was communal in character and had a pan-Islamic content'. He then proceeds (p. 129) to say, rightly, that 'there is no record of any Muslim violence against the Hindus' and so 'we cannot dismiss the Talla riot as one caused merely by Muslim community-consciousness and pan-Islamism'. (The word 'dismiss' is of course symptomatic of Das Gupta's standpoint. Why must we 'dismiss' a communal riot? Surely, even a communal riot needs explaining?)

But did I ever describe the Talla riot as 'communal'? Nowhere in the pages of CRL that Das Gupta has referred to (pp. 49–50, 53–4, 58) do I use the word 'communal' to describe the Talla riot. 'Communal' was a word that I had expressly reserved in CRL (p. 5) for cases of '*overt* Hindu–Muslim tension', and the Talla riot was not a case of Hindu–Muslim conflict. But surely it originated around Muslim-community-centered demands, Muslims surely formed a majority among the rioters, and rumours afloat during the riot surely show a pan-Islamist content. The aforementioned pages of CRL give enough evidence to make these points and I have no hesitation in standing by them.

These specific misreadings are themselves indicative of a broader misreading: Das Gupta obviously misunderstood my category of 'community consciousness' to mean that the workers were 'intrinsically communal' (see pp. 78–80) and that the Hindus and Muslims were always out for each other's blood. In CRL, the problem at hand was to understand the relationship between the Hindu-Muslim conflicts of 1896 and the jute mill working class. The question at the centre of the essay was: Why were communal riots a possibility in the mill working-class milieu? Das Gupta's argument that there were only three such riots is totally besides the point.[5] To quote what he himself says in a slightly different context: 'What is of particular significance here is not so much the extent of these actions as their character' (p. 123).

In trying to understand the 'significance' of these riots, I looked at the years before and after 1896, that is, 1894–5 and 1897, and saw a continuity. This was the continued existence of what I called 'community consciousness'. In the rather-too-apologetic 'introduction' to the Occasional Paper version of CRL, I defined community consciousness to mean 'a state of mind whereby a Muslim worker thinks of himself primarily as a Muslim, or the Hindu of himself firstly as a Hindu' (p. 5). That is to say, it referred to a consciousness to which religion was of crucial importance, and for which religion was a means of ordering the world. I used 'communal', as I have already said, to indicate *overt* Hindu–Muslim conflicts (CRL, p. 5). In other words, communal conflicts were an articulation of community consciousness, but they also included a degree of intolerance for people outside the community—something that I did *not* see as a necessary attribute of community consciousness, as I had defined the term.

Why is Das Gupta so dismissive of the communal riots of 1896? The question gains additional importance in view of the fact that, while (see Das Gupta, p. 142) there was not even a single strike in which all the workers of a mill combined, not to speak of inter-mill combinations, all the riots mentioned saw labourers from different mills participating in them. Das Gupta's blind spot is created by his idea of class consciousness that he opposes to my category of community consciousness. Let me quote Das Gupta here *in extenso* on class consciousness, for the point is crucial:

It may be stated that the workers in the 1890s were haltingly discovering ... certain elementary rules and truth[s] about class warfare ... (p. 149). ... Thus here was the birth of *class feeling* [original emphasis]—a feeling of an identity of interests as between the workers themselves and as against the employers ... in defending as well as advancing its immediate interests, the *transitional* [original emphasis] workforce *was trying* [my emphasis], of course in a rambling and sporadic fashion, to overcome its part human ... condition of existence, to establish working class and thus human rights and *to get on the road, towards self awareness and working class consciousness* [my emphasis] (p. 150).

Inspiring words—but we must admit, a rather tortuous imagery. The point is *not* stylistic, as the imagery invoked is quite in keeping with Das Gupta's idea of class consciousness. For, 'trying to get on the road etc.' assumes an important awareness on the part of the proletariat: that such a road exists, and the road indeed is *the* proletarian highway to class consciousness. This is a pointer to one important aspect of Das Gupta's handling of the category of class consciousness. For him, it is not an open-ended, problematical phenomenon. It is an *automatic* result of the capitalist mode of production. The working class anywhere is born with an instinct for moving towards class consciousness. It is the sense of this 'movement' that Das Gupta packs into the expression '*transitional* workforce'. Indeed, his workers '*discover* [my emphasis] ... rules and truth of class warfare'—rules and truths that were obviously already there—by the very fact of being workers, so great is their 'epistemological privilege'. Das Gupta clearly sees 'the *instinct* [my emphasis] of rebellion against capitalist exploitation—writ large' over their actions.

Such an 'instinctive' view of class consciousness—a class consciousness that spontaneously results from the objective position of the proletariat itself—can only be ahistorical. It exists by separating the *concrete* history of labour from the *concrete* history of capital. This becomes clear if we follow closely Das Gupta's argument.

Das Gupta seems to have a three-step argument with respect to the phenomenon of class consciousness. The first step states that first-generation workers *in all countries* exhibit certain *similar* forms of pre-capitalist behaviour and mental attitudes:

> It should be noted that the sort of responses referred to above was not peculiar to factory workers of Bengal or India in the seventies and eighties of the last century. That in the classic British case and in the *initial period of all the industrialising countries* [my emphasis] the early workers behaved by and large in a similar fashion is too well known to merit any repetition here.[6]

The second step states that what really makes a 'class' of this mass of factory workers by developing class consciousness in their minds is intensive industrialization:

> But in Britain (and other industrializing countries of the nineteenth century), such problems were transient in history ... the elements of pre-capitalist habits of mind and behaviour, in the worker's attitudes or in the total social structure, were transcended through the cumulative progress of the Industrial Revolution which accounted for the transformation of workers into a working class within the broader society, and also for the growth of working class consciousness and action, ethos and culture.[7]

The third step, then, is to argue that in the Indian case, because 'genuine capitalist industrialisation was ruled out by the colonial order', it is 'no wonder that even second or third generation workers remained rootless, part human, half proletarian, wretched creatures' (p. 28). Thus, it may be noted that the kind of activities in which the worker in England or France or Germany in the early period of industrialization participated or the economic, political, social outlook exhibited by them or the type of organization they formed are not to be found here (Bengal). The colonialized character of the industrial situation ruled these out (p. 150).

So, if the working class here did not show class consciousness, the blame, in this analysis, lies squarely with colonialism. For, as Das Gupta says, the workers, on their own were, of course, 'trying … to get on the road towards … working class consciousness'. They even had 'class feelings' against their employers. Yet 'it was not … class consciousness' (p. 150), because the colonial laboratory where the working class was being made lacked the crucial reagent of an industrial revolution, so important for the precipitation of such consciousness!

There is, may I say, a profoundly mistaken reading here of E.P. Thompson. Thompson clearly says:

The making of the working class is a fact of political and cultural, as much as of economic, history. It was not the spontaneous generation of the factory system. Nor should we think of an external force—the 'industrial revolution'—working upon some nondescript undifferentiated raw material of humanity, and turning it out at the other end as a 'fresh race of beings'. … the Industrial Revolution

… [was] imposed, not upon raw material, but upon the free-born Englishman—and the free-born Englishman as Paine had left him or as the Methodists had moulded him. The factory hand or stockinger was also the inheritor of Bunyan, of remembered village rights, of notions of equality before the law, of craft traditions. He was the object of massive religious indoctrination and the creator of political traditions. *The working class made itself as much as it was made.*[8]

Thus, for E.P. Thompson, the making of the English working class takes place in the context both of the Industrial Revolution and the actual cultural and political traditions that the working class inherits from its empirical past. But not so for Das Gupta. True, he spends a few pages (see pp. 134–41) discussing 'religious holiday demands', but for him, religion is either a mere psychological prop for the uprooted migrant or a source of entertainment in the drab life of the labourer or simply a 'language' for protest. (Das Gupta underscores the last formulation.) It is never a part of a world outlook. He overlooks the specific nature of religion here. He does not stop to think how the specific cultural past of the jute worker relates to the question of class consciousness. His lack of interest in the specific leads him to draw a parallel again with the history of the English working class—a parallel quite superficial and unwarranted. Das Gupta writes, 'in the absence of any alternative ideology and programme, the factory workers (here) were compelled to turn towards traditional custom and religion. *Their aspirations and protests were clothed in religious language, fashions and forms* [original emphasis]. In early nineteenth century Britain too the initial protests of the raw workers took religious forms' (pp. 137–8).

Two points need to be made about this supposed similarity between the two histories. Firstly, there is very little in common between the relationship among religion, working class, and capitalism in England and that here. E.P. Thompson, for example, writes about the 'double service' that Methodism performed for the Industrial Revolution. It became a religion both of the bourgeoisie and the working class; it was instrumental in the development of work-discipline in the factories.[9] Founding dissenting, working-class sects there was often a matter of getting out of employer-controlled churches.[10] There is no such relationship between Islam or Hinduism and colonial capitalism in Bengal.

Secondly, to the extent the early English working class displayed class consciousness, the articulation of that consciousness was not religious. The English model does not provide us a basis for equating class consciousness with religion. The state of knowledge in this regard was thus summarized ten years ago by a well-known Marxist historian:

> It is naturally to the world of the artisan that historians have turned in attempting to define the metropolitan radical and socialist tradition. This world has been finely evoked in recent works by Eric Hobsbawm, Edward Thompson, Gwyn Williams, and Royden Harrison ... *The texture of this artisan radicalism was secular rather than religious, rational rather than inspirational.* Its spiritual forefathers were the Levellers, Paine, Volney and Voltaire.[11]

Yet Das Gupta constantly uses the rhetoric of *The Making* without using its problematic. His workforce is 'transitional', it is in 'the process of becoming a working class' (p. 141), his Talla riots are comparable to E.P. Thompson's Gordon riots,[12] his 'sophisticated' disapproval of my term 'community consciousness' comparable to Thompson's of the term

'riot'.[13] Even his formulation on 'class feeling'
echoes strongly that of Thompson's on
class consciousness, and I will quote them
both here:

> **Das Gupta:** 'Thus here was the birth of class-
> feeling—a feeling of an identity of interest
> as between the workers themselves and as
> against the employers' (p. 150).

> **Thompson:** 'The period between 1790 and
> 1830 ... [saw] the growth of class consciousness:
> the consciousness of an identity of interest as
> between all the diverse groups of working
> people and as against the interest of other
> classes' (p. 212).

Both the similarities and the differences
between the two formulations are striking.
Thompson's phrase 'all the diverse groups of
working people' is dropped in Das Gupta's
formulation—I suppose it is one way of
avoiding the problems that religion, caste,
and other primordial loyalties pose; and the
word 'consciousness' is replaced by the word
'feeling'. This replacement is interesting,
for it enables Das Gupta to add that it 'was
not yet class consciousness'. But does that
improve matters? If the workers *felt* an
identity of interests between themselves and

against their employers, weren't they, for all practical purposes, class conscious—unless Das Gupta is referring to the kind of hatred and hostility that the urban poor often reserve for the rich?[14] Can this 'class feeling' be really inferred from documents? Isn't Das Gupta smuggling in 'class consciousness' through the back door? And if he is, does it not contradict his own argument that we need the Industrial Revolution to transform pre-capitalist attitudes into class attitudes? How did it all happen here in the course of a few years—for Das Gupta's workers were showing pre-capitalist attitudes even in the 1880s—without the Industrial Revolution intervening? The answer, in his terms, can only be sustained by using some ahistorical category of class consciousness such as he has produced in his paper.

Yet, to be fair to Das Gupta, he is not alone in investing 'class consciousness' with some degree of automaticity. He belongs to a tradition of historiography in India. Among recent authors writing on the Indian working class, Sukomal Sen and Panchanan Saha have come up with very similar ideas.[15] For them, as for Das Gupta, protest becomes equal to class consciousness—in other words, no distinction is made between class struggle and class identity—and nothing mediates between the economic/objective position of the worker and the generation of such consciousness. The actual, empirical consciousness of the worker hardly gets a notice in the hands of these authors, both the 'growth' and 'retardation' of class consciousness being explainable solely in terms of economic exploitation. Consider, for instance, Sen's formulation on class consciousness, which is very close to what I have described as Das Gupta's three-step argument: 'Class-consciousness of the proletariat, as a general rule, rises in proportion to the advance of economic struggles against capitalist exploitation. But in a colony, some specific features of exploitation as distinct from that in a metropolitan country, impede the development of economic struggles of the workers and in consequence retard the growth of their class political consciousness.'[16]

But then, again, Sen alone is not to blame; for long before him, there was R.P. Dutt (whom Saha quotes with approval) who, in his trail-blazing *India Today* (1946), left a framework that later Indian Marxists have often blindly accepted. The following quotation from Dutt will make clear how similar his, Sen's, and Das Gupta's concerns are:

> For the early history of the Indian labour movement it would be necessary to piece together the records of the strike movement from the eighties onwards in the documents of the period. Although there was not yet any organisation, it would be a mistake to underestimate the growth of solidarity in action and elementary class consciousness of Indian industrial workers ... [before] 1914.[17]

We are thus all heirs (or prisoners, shall I say), within Marxism, to ways of thinking about class consciousness. One of these traditions seems to postulate an extra-historical rationality (and hence class consciousness) that can indeed be read into the actions of the working class anywhere. It seems to me that insofar as we want to make the writing of Indian labour history a serious, intellectual proposition—and this will have implications for our political practice—this particular aspect of our heritage needs to be seriously re-examined. A brief excursion, at this point, into some theoretical considerations may help clarify the issue.

One can identify four moments in the development of Marxism when the question of class consciousness received attention: in early Marx (two key texts being *Poverty of Philosophy* and *The Holy Family*), Lenin's *What Is to Be Done?* (1902), Lukács' *History and Class Consciousness* (1922/3), and in the writings of Gramsci. I shall skip early Marx, for some of the problems that his category of class consciousness poses for the practising historian have already been noted.

The couplet 'alienation/class consciousness' derives from early Marx. Consciousness, in this sense, implies the recuperation of an alienated essence. As is well known, Marx derived this schema from an application and extension of the Feuerbachian critique of Hegel. The moment of consciousness here is not historical, but ontological. It appeals to a moment of absolute truth, to which no concrete historical process could ever aspire. Indeed, this is its most obvious defect; that—quite apart from other epistemological objections which could be raised against it—it bears only the most notional and abstract relation to material history.[18]

I shall also skip Lenin. For two reasons: (*a*) the 'formidable difficulties' that historians may face in applying Leninist categories to concrete historical situations are very well brought out in Gareth Stedman Jones's review of John Foster;[19] and (*b*) the philosophical foundations for Lenin's views were really worked out by Lukács whose idea of class consciousness I discuss below.

With Lukács, we come to a rigorously analysed concept of class consciousness, which is indeed ahistorical and universal, but a concept that has very little to do with what actually goes on in people's minds in specific historical junctures. Class consciousness, for Lukács, consists of 'the ideas, sentiments, etc., which men in a given situation of life *would* have, *if they were able to grasp in its entirety* this situation, and the interests deriving from it, both as regards immediate action and as regards the structure of society which (would) correspond to those interests'.[20] Thus, class consciousness consists, in fact, of the appropriate and rational reactions '*imputed*' [my emphasis] ... to a particular typical position in the process of production. *This consciousness is ... neither the sum nor the average of what is or felt by the single individuals who make up the class* [my emphasis].[21]

As the editors of the English translation of *History and Class Consciousness* explain, Lukács' 'imputed' consciousness is a logical category; it refers 'neither to the actual consciousness of a class, nor to the consciousness it ought really to have'.[22] Class consciousness, for Lukács, is completely separate from the 'empirically given'. More important, there is *no* passage between the two; we cannot pass from one to the other. He makes this clear in his comments on Marx's remarks regarding 'the revolt of the Silesian weavers'. Discussing Mehring's question of whether Marx did not overestimate the weavers' consciousness, Lukács writes: 'The unique element in its [the working class's] situation is that its surpassing of immediacy represents an aspiration towards society in its totality *regardless of* [my emphasis] whether this aspiration remains conscious or whether it remains unconscious for the moment.'[23]

One may or may not agree with Lukács in his 1919–23 phase, but it is easy to see that his concept of class consciousness is not of much help to the historian writing about what goes on within people's heads. This is why Hobsbawm, in his aforementioned article on Lukács, quickly takes leave of the master by saying, 'I shall ... leave aside much of Lukács's discussion as irrelevant to my purpose, which is the rather modest one of a historian.'[24] Some of the historian's problems with the Lukácsian standpoint, as well as those envisaged from a broader perspective, have been effectively put forward by Richard Johnson:

> Lukács remains important for his concentration on consciousness, for his criticisms of an unreflexive epistemology ... But he is also a classical instance of two recurrent tendencies ...: the tendency to see class cultures as straightforwardly and wholly conditioned by social position (for this is the argument, ultimately, about class consciousness); and the tendency to ascribe to whole societies one 'central' or 'essential' modality of thought which enters the consciousness of all classes (for this is the argument about 'false consciousness'). The major fatality, as always in the class/class consciousness problematic, is any concrete, complex account of lived cultures, how they are formed and how they may be transformed.[25]

I chose to discuss Lukács because his seemed the best exposition of an ahistorical idea of class consciousness, an idea logically pursued in an extremely rigorous analysis. Of course, Das Gupta does not use an explicitly Lukácsian concept, nor do Panchanan Saha or Sukomal Sen. Their intellectual premises, as we have seen, go back to Lenin's *What Is to Be Done?*, or nearer in time, to R.P. Dutt. But Dutt's was also an ahistorical, acultural notion of class consciousness, as it was employed within the Stalinist tradition. The point emerging from our discussion of Lukács was that you could not both sustain an ahistorical concept of class consciousness and at the same time write a working-class history using what E.P. Thompson has recently called 'the empirical idiom'. Lukács, of course, was aware of this and divorced his concept from empirical history. But Das Gupta wants to marry the two and, no wonder, ends up contradicting himself at several places. To mention only a few:

- Das Gupta's workers show 'indifference to work' in the 1880s (pp. 25, 28). But a few years later, to the Factory Commission of 1890, they, in fact, show their 'willingness to work' (p. 43). Das Gupta has no problem explaining this. The former shows the worker's 'instinct of rebellion against capitalist exploitation', while the latter 'reveals an important attribute of ... industrial workers ... which was [so] much different from the attitude of beggars ...'!

- Das Gupta (p. 32) explicitly 'associate[s]' strikes 'with the industrial proletariat' yet in the same breath mentions (p. 31, n. 70) 'early strikes of the non-industrial labouring men' of Calcutta, long before even the modern factories came up.

- By Das Gupta's own admission, the jute mill workers were 'nothing but casual labour' (p. 143). Yet this seems to have posed no problems for either their 'discovering' the 'rules' of 'class warfare' or for their 'striving' to get on to 'the road' to class consciousness.

The trouble is that both Das Gupta and the provider of his kind of framework, R.P. Dutt, seem to be writing history in terms of inspiring present-day struggles. Which is why both of them—and others in the same tradition—are anxious not to 'belittle' or 'underestimate' (see Das Gupta, p. 150 and Dutt quoted above) the historical 'significance' of working-class actions. The purpose of writing history, from this standpoint, can only be to provide contemporary labour movements with their 'myths'—that is, to mythologize the past.[26] This may be a valid political gesture, but does not help the historian in dealing with his facts. In this, I can do no better than quote

Hobsbawm: 'To dip into the past for inspiring examples of struggle or the like is to write history backwards and eclectically. It is not a very good way of writing it.'[27]

But does that mean that Marxist historians of 'consciousness' are condemned to writing 'bad' history? Or to put it another way, is 'good' history of 'consciousness' of no use to Marxist political practice? This is where Gramsci's thoughts seem to point a way out of the closedness of Lukácsian formulations. For Gramsci, what goes on in the minds of people is important even in his philosophical framework; he argues from the premise that 'each man ... is a "philosopher" ... he participates in a particular conception of the world ... and therefore contributes to sustain ... that conception ... or to modify it, that is to bring into being new modes of thought'.[28]

So if hegemony has to be won for proletarian ideology, Marxism has to establish real relationships of exchange with the actual, empirical consciousness of people. It should be possible, in other words, to pass from one to the other. Gramsci writes:

Can modern theory [Marxism] be in opposition to the 'spontaneous' feelings of the

masses? ('Spontaneous' in the sense that they
… have been formed … by the traditional
popular conception of the world—what is
unimaginatively called 'instinct'). It cannot
be in opposition to them. Between the two
there is a quantitative difference of degree, so
to speak, a passage from one to the other and
vice versa, must be possible.[29]

And again: 'The unity between "spontaneity"
and "conscious" leadership or "discipline"
is precisely the real political action of the
subaltern classes, insofar as this is mass politics
and not merely an adventure by groups
claiming to represent the masses.'[30]

The last quotation shows that Gramsci's
is a position in favour of non-substitutionist
politics. The organizational imperatives of such
politics have not been worked out yet, and
much of Marxist thinking on organizational
problems to date remains deeply Leninist,
the philosophical premises of which were set
out by Lukács.[31] But if a socially hegemonic
role for the proletarian ideology is seen as an
important objective of political practice, such
practice will need to be based on some of the
Gramscian premises.

It then becomes necessary, as Gramsci said,
'to study and develop the elements of popular

psychology, historically and sociologically, active (i.e. in order to transform them by educating them into a modern mentality)'.[32] And the historian is free, once again, to be both a Marxist and a historian, and yet not mythologize history. My research on the jute mill workers of Bengal shows that religion, caste, or 'community' continued to remain important to them at least till 1940 (where my study ends) and even later. And there are times when these factors act as real dividers of the working class. Some of the first 'battles' of the 1946 Hindu–Muslim riot, for example, were fought in the jute mills. A 'conspiracy' theory does not help, nor does a crude idea of 'false consciousness'—and they both take real, actual, living people for fools.[33] We need categories that can handle the existence of issues like caste or religion (or the like) in the minds of people, and also help explain their continued existence. My category of 'community consciousness' was a response to this need. I saw 'community' as an ensemble of relationships one is born into, as opposed to 'class', which is based on an associational principle.[34] It may have been an imperfect category. But the alternative category of an ahistorical, acultural, and automatic 'class consciousness' simply will not serve.

Notes and References

* I am grateful to Barun De, Anthony Low, and Tapan Raychaudhuri for criticisms of an earlier draft. Partha Chatterjee and Roger Stuart have acted as excellent sounding boards for testing out ideas. All remaining follies are results of my own shortcomings.

  This note is also written in the belief that the ideas I criticize here are widely shared by leftist historians of the Indian working class. So, engaging in a debate with Das Gupta will, I hope, have a relevance broader than that which is merely personal. In structuring this note, however, I start with Das Gupta's specific criticisms of my work, and from there try to work my way towards some questions of wider interest.

1. E.P. Thompson, *Social History* 3, no. 2 (May 1978).

2. See Ranajit Das Gupta, 'Material Conditions and Behavioural Aspects of Calcutta Working Class 1875–1899' (Occasional Paper 22, Centre for Studies in Social Sciences [CSSSC], Calcutta, January 1979) and my paper, Dipesh Chakrabarty, 'Communal Riots and Labour: Bengal's Jute Mill Hands in the 1890s,' (Occasional Paper 11, Centre for Studies in Social Sciences, Calcutta, 1976). 'Communal Riots and Labour' (CRL) has had two versions. In its first incarnation, it was circulated as

the Occasional Paper 11 of the CSSSC; in its second and much revised form, it is awaiting publication in *Past and Present*. Since Das Gupta's references are to the Occasional Paper version, and since none of my later revisions would take me any closer to his position than I was before, all references to CRL in this note are to its 'first incarnation'.

3. See also my paper 'On Deifying and Defying Authority: Managers and Workers in Bengal Jute Mills c. 1890–1940' to be published in Ranajit Guha, ed., *Subaltern Studies*, vol. II.

4. Hossainur Rahman, *Hindu–Muslim Relations in Bengal 1905–1947* (Bombay: Nachiketa, 1974). See Appendices (pp. 153–4) where a letter written by Zahiruddin Ahmad is reproduced.

5. My later research indicates that there were more such riots. There is at least one very important file in the West Bengal State Archives (in the pre-1901 section), which I had unfortunately overlooked at the time of writing CRL. Most of the files, however, have been destroyed.

6. Das Gupta, 'Material Conditions and Behavioural Aspects of Calcutta Working Class,' 26–7.

7. Das Gupta, 'Material Conditions and Behavioural Aspects of Calcutta Working Class,' 27; the reference here is to, among others, E.P. Thompson's *The Making of the English Working Class*.

8. E.P. Thompson, *The Making of the English Working Class* (1963; Harmondsworth: Penguin Books, 1968), p. 213, my emphasis.

9. Thompson, *The Making of the English Working Class*, 391–3.

10. See, for example, John Foster, *Class Struggle and the Industrial Revolution* (1974; London: Methuen & Co. Ltd, 1977), 30–1.

11. Gareth Stedman Jones, *Outcast London* (Oxford: Oxford University Press, 1971), 339. Emphasis added.

12. Compare the following:

    • Das Gupta, 'Material Conditions and Behavioural Aspects of Calcutta Working Class,' 132, on the Talla riots: 'was a kind of mixture of a mob ... sought to be operated by ... external interest (that is, a "manipulated" mob—Dipesh Chakrabarty [DC]) and a crowd spontaneously rebelling....'

    • Thompson, *The Making of the English Working Class*, 78: 'We have here ... something of a mixture of manipulated mob and revolutionary crowd.'

13. Compare:

    • Das Gupta, 'Material Conditions and Behavioural Aspects of Calcutta Working Class,' 137: 'It (the demand for festival holidays—DC) was legitimised by more sophisticated traditions than a term like "community consciousness" suggests.'

- Thompson, *The Making of the English Working Class*, 67: 'It [riotous action—DC] … was validated by more sophisticated traditions than the word "riot" suggests.'

14. See Jones, *Outcast London*, 342. Jones, however, clearly distinguishes such casual labour-urban poor radicalism from artisan 'class consciousness'. 'The suggestion [the reference here is to G. Rudé, *The Crowd in History* (New York: John Wiley & Sons, 1964), 221] that ideas like "the rights of man" or "the sovereignty of the people" began to permeate the consciousness of the metropolitan poor from the French Revolution onwards, finds little echo in the existing evidence…'

15. Sukomal Sen, *Working Class of India: History of Emergence and Movement, 1830–1970* (Calcutta: K.P. Bagchi, 1977) and Panchanan Saha, *History of the Working-Class Movement in Bengal* (New Delhi: People's Publishing House, 1978).

16. Sen, *Working Class of India*, 87.

17. R.P. Dutt, *India Today* (Bombay: People's Publishing House, 1946), 331, quoted in Saha, preface to *History of the Working-Class Movement in Bengal*, 1.

18. Gareth Stedman Jones, 'Class Struggle and the Industrial Revolution' [a review essay

on Foster's book by the same title], *New Left Review* I, no. 90 (March–April 1975): 47.

19. Jones, 'Class Struggle and the Industrial Revolution,' 47–8.

20. Georg Lukács, *History and Class Consciousness* (London: Merlin Press, 1971), 51. I have, however, used Hobsbawm's translation of this sentence, as given in E.J. Hobsbawm, 'Class Consciousness in History' in *Aspects of History and Class Consciousness*, ed. István Mészáros (London: Routledge & Kegan Paul, 1971), 6.

21. Lukács, *History and Class Consciousness*, 51.

22. Lukács, *History and Class Consciousness*, 345.

23. Lukács, *History and Class Consciousness*, 174, 219.

24. Hobsbawm, 'Class Consciousness', 7.

25. Richard Johnson, 'Three Problematics: Elements of a Theory of Working-class Culture' in *Working-Class Culture: Studies in History and Theory*, eds. John Clarke, Chas Critcher, and Richard Johnson (London: Hutchinson, 1979), 211.

26. This, I think, is one reason why a serious tradition of labour history has not developed in India so far.

27. E.J. Hobsbawm, 'Labour History and Ideology,' *Journal of Social History* 7, no. 4 (Summer 1974): 375.

28. Q. Hoare and G.N. Smith, eds and trans., *Selections from the Prison Notebooks of Antonio*

Gramsci (New York: International Publishers, 1973), 9.

29. Hoare and Smith, *Selections from the Prison Notebooks of Antonio Gramsci*, 198–9.

30. Hoare and Smith, *Selections from the Prison Notebooks of Antonio Gramsci*, 198.

31. Gramsci's position is based on the (problematic) assumption that consciousness can indeed be changed by purposeful intervention. There is also the point that substitutionist politics may, in fact, be the more feasible alternative in a country like India in the short-term future, at least insofar as raising people's standards of living and capturing state-power are concerned. These are important considerations but they need not detain us here.

32. Gramsci quoted in Johnson, 'Three Problematics,' 209.

33. Compare with E.P. Thompson, *Whigs and Hunters* (Harmondsworth: Penguin Books, 1977), 262: '... people are not as stupid as some structuralist [Thompson's unfortunate term for 'Stalinism' in modern intellection—DC] philosophers suppose them to be. They will not be mystified by the first man who puts on a wig.' For Thompson's critique of 'structuralism', see his 'The Poverty of Theory' in E.P. Thompson, *The Poverty of Theory and Other Essays* (London: Merlin Press, 1978).

34. For a theoretical discussion of the problem, see Partha Chatterjee, 'Thinking about Ideology: In Search of an Analytical Framework' (Occasional Paper 21, Centre for Studies in Social Sciences, Calcutta, November 1978), 7–10.

2. A Reply

Ranajit Das Gupta

I am grateful to Dipesh Chakrabarty for his critique of my 'Material Conditions and Behavioural Aspects of Calcutta Working Class 1875–1899' (hereafter Occasional Paper 22). His sharply critical tone notwithstanding, I am sure his poser of certain important issues will contribute to a better understanding of labour history in colonial India and also of Marxism as a method of investigating and analysing that history.

At the outset, I must admit that, at several places of my Occasional Paper, the language and style are not happy. I also must admit that, in one or two places, Chakrabarty has caught me at my weak spots. He has taken exception to my ascribing to him the position that he picked out a passage from the Government of Bengal's reply to the 1892 Royal Commission on Labour to prove the absence of open and direct action on the part of workers in the 1880s. I agree that this is certainly not his explicitly stated position. But it must also be emphasized that there is not a single reference in his Occasional Paper to any of the several open and direct actions of the workers that took place in the 1870s and 1880s.

Despite Chakrabarty's hard-hitting criticism, I find no reason to revise my basic position. Chakrabarty's essential contention that the workers in the 1890s were only community-conscious and, at times, even communal and did not exhibit any working-class attitude and characteristics is in my view absolutely wrong. The disagreement arises from fundamental differences of perspective, method, handling of materials, and analysis. In this reply, I am going to limit myself to those disagreements that may be discussed fruitfully. Acrimony, in however smart and elegant a prose style, is not only infructuous but tiresome as well.

My central concern has been to study the process of transformation of sections of the labouring population into an industrial working class in late-nineteenth-century Bengal. This was a complex social process full of zigzags and contradictions. In the paper, my focus has been on the formation of the proletariat (Occasional

Paper 22, pp. 7–8), and their conditions of work and existence as well as their mental and behavioural response to such conditions in a colonial setting.

In doing that study, I have touched on certain aspects of Dipesh Chakrabarty's paper. I have found his intention to go 'beyond the bounds of conventional labour history and venture into the field of urban and political histories' to be a line of enquiry full of promise. But, in practice, his central and only focus is unambiguously indicated by the title of his paper: 'Communal Riots and Labour'. His area of interest is considerably different from and, so far as the above-mentioned paper is concerned, much narrower than that of mine. Chakrabarty neither sees labour history as a historical process nor indicates any awareness of the immense complexities involved in the unfolding of such a historical process.

In the context of such an approach, it is not surprising that he implies that there is a contradiction (Critique, p. 3)[1] between my observations that it is 'factually erroneous' to speak about 'the absence of workers' open and direct action' in the 1870s and 1880s (Occasional Paper 22, p. 33) and that 'the period from 1880s to mid-1890s was one of lull' (Occasional Paper 22, p. 38). But the same passage, which Chakrabarty quotes (Critique, p. 4), mentions 'the battles of the early 1880s' (Occasional Paper 22, pp. 32–8). Chakrabarty fails to comprehend that the history of workers' action is not a history of linear progression. The early stirrings among factory workers in Bengal were followed by a few years of quiescence. But this was temporary. Soon workers' action began to take place in much greater frequency and intensity than before. I have tried to chronicle as well as analyse the significance of these actions. If there are any apparent contradictions in my paper, then they arise from the contradictory developments and processes to be found in the actual happenings of history. The problem here is not any internal contradictions in my argument, but Chakrabarty's attempts to ignore all happenings that do not fit in with his stereotype of the community-conscious worker.

Chakrabarty accuses me of 'misreading' and at times of 'misrepresentation' (Critique, p. 2). He is indignant with me for finding his 'Communal Riots and Labour' 'somewhat exaggerated', for holding him responsible for 'belittling' 'the significance' of the jute workers' struggle in the 1890s, for considering his term 'community consciousness' too narrow

(Critique, p. 2), and for accusing him of arguing that the Talla riot was 'communal in character and pan-Islamic in content', (Critique, p. 5). It is true that he draws a distinction between the two categories 'community consciousness' and 'communal outlook'. Also true, he does not explicitly characterize the Talla riot as 'communal'. But his Occasional Paper gives the clear impression that his sole concern is with the communal aspects of workers' feelings and attitudes and also with only those riots that were communal. The very title of his paper—'Communal Riots and Labour'—does not leave any scope for ambiguity regarding his central focus.[2]

In course of his argument and analysis in 'Communal Riots and Labour', the definitional distinction drawn between 'community consciousness' and 'communal attitude', a distinction about which he speaks so much in his critique, gets blurred and the two categories become interchangeable. Thus, he speaks of 'rioting by mill hands on ... communal issues, or of the growth of "community consciousness" among some jute mill hands' (CRL, p. 19). Spelling out his objective, he writes, 'We are for the [sic] beginnings of certain social trends, e.g. trends of communal tension among labouring men in Calcutta' (CRL, p. 6). He adds, 'We have *selected* data with *this objective* in mind' (CRL, p. 6; [emphasis mine]). In view of all this, is it misleading to consider his category of 'community consciousness' as synonymous with 'communal outlook'? Considering the fact that he has chosen to disregard all those aspects of the Talla riot which show that it was much more than only a religious, communal, and pan-Islamic riot, am I to be faulted for suggesting that, in Chakrabarty's view, the Talla riot was just a 'communal and pan-Islamic' riot?

Chakrabarty asks in a tone of disapprobation: 'Why is Das Gupta so dismissive of the communal riots of 1896?' (Critique, p. 7). But am I really so dismissive? I have made two pointed and specific references to these riots in two places (Occasional Paper 22, pp. 80–1 and 119–20), with due acknowledgement to Chakrabarty himself. But I had no wish to repeat the discussion made by Chakrabarty. I also wanted to view these riots in the overall context of labour discontent, violent action, and even criminal practices on the part of the workers in the late nineteenth century.

Chakrabarty, however, takes a different view. He concentrates on the communal violence to the virtual exclusion of all other kinds of group action. This is nothing but a highly one-sided and misleading treatment of communal riots, particularly when, to go by even Chakrabarty's own account in his Occasional Paper, there were only three incidents of the former kind; while the number of open and direct actions, such as mass deputations, strikes, and crowd violence in the 1890s around industrial issues in defence of their interests at the department or factory level, were no less than 14.

Chakrabarty's reference to archival and newspaper sources indicates that he must have come across at least some of the relevant evidence, which is also quoted extensively in my paper. Yet, after making a mention of these actions in a most perfunctory manner, it is he who chooses to take, to use his own term, a 'dismissive' view of all protest actions and industrial struggles against capitalist employers—all actions that cut across religious community boundaries. In fact, he himself makes the admission: 'Our sample of riots is … biased' (CRL, p. 3). Again: 'This paper also suffers from a lopsided emphasis' (CRL, p. 5). What Chakrabarty describes as 'biased' and 'lopsided', I prefer to call 'exaggerated'.

What is involved in all this is not just belittling of the 'significance' of workers' action but something more. There is a total disregard for workers' collective action against capitalist employers. In his critique, he is full of self-righteous injunctions about writing '*concrete* history of labour' (Critique, p. 9, emphasis in the original), 'empirical history' (Critique, p. 8), and 'good' and 'bad' history (Critique, p. 20). It is indeed unfortunate that Chakrabarty's own way of writing 'concrete history of labour' and 'empirical history' consists in ignoring all awkward facts.

The argument in my paper has not been that the early jute workers never exhibited community-centric attitudes or at times were not embroiled in communal riots. The argument has been that they were not merely communal or community-centric but that they also put forward demands and resorted to mass actions which reflected, despite various limitations, their efforts to bring about some improvement in their conditions of work and living. Similarly, the argument has not been that the demand for festival holidays did not indicate any 'community consciousness'. The argument has been that the category 'community consciousness' is not adequate for understanding the demand for festival holidays, which in my view 'reflected the desperate striving of the raw and new workers to recreate the old way of life on an adapted basis' and 'also a protest by the raw workers .... against the new kind of oppression and exploitation they faced' (Occasional Paper 22, p. 137).

Chakrabarty does not either question the evidence or refute my line of reasoning. He simply makes certain assertions. With regard to the Kankinarah Mahomedan Association and the Talla riot, he makes an attempt to present some sort of logic. In my paper, I have argued that though the Association in its early days (that is, about 1895) was just a philanthropic organization looking after the interests of Muslim workers only, soon there was a change in its composition as well as nature of activities. Thus, Kazi Zahir-ud-din Ahmed, the president of the association, in his evidence submitted to the Indian Factory Labour Commission of 1908 stated, 'It [the Association] was started in 1895 with the object of attracting more Mahomedans to jute mills, but since then Hindus had been admitted to membership, and now the Association looked after the interests of the operatives generally....' He informed the commission that, in preparing his representation, he had 'consulted a good number of representative Hindu and Musalman workers'. And he asked for holidays on account of both Muslim and Hindu religious festivals.[3] Chakrabarty, however, mentions only that portion of Zahir-ud-din's evidence that seems to buttress his argument but leaves out all that contradicts his thesis. In his Critique (p. 4 and f.n. 3), he refers to a piece of evidence, a letter written by Zahir-ud-din to the private secretary to the Viceroy, which purports to establish that he was pro-British and anti-Hindu. This letter, written at the height of the Swadeshi movement, shows that he certainly exhibited a loyalist attitude and was opposed to the Swadeshi movement, which he thought was led by some Calcutta-based Hindu zamindars. But does this establish that the Mahomedan Association was an organization of Muslim workers only and looked after their interests only? Further, have I argued that the Mahomedan Association of which Zahir-ud-din was president was an anti-British and militantly anti-capitalist organization? What I have argued is that the activities and various demands, including the demand for religious festival holidays, had much wider implications. But Chakrabarty stubbornly refuses to see the significance of the fact that Zahir-ud-din, despite his loyalist stance, was not averse to opening the doors of the association to Hindu workers, holding joint meetings of Hindu and Muslim workers, and putting forward demands for Muslim as well as Hindu festival holidays. He also doggedly refuses to see the underlying incipient labour-capital conflict in all this.

With regard to the Talla riot, Chakrabarty complacently reiterates, 'surely it originated around Muslim-community-centered demands, Muslims surely formed a majority among the rioters, and rumours afloat during the riot surely show a pan-Islamist content'. On the basis of evidence that I could gather, I have contended in my paper, 'the Talla riot had its anomaly. This was because of its narrow Muslim-centred origin and pan-Islamic overtone on the one hand and its broad popular anti-police, anti-Government direction on the other' (Occasional Paper 22, pp. 131–2). I do not still know whether Chakrabarty agrees with these findings and observations.

Chakrabarty deliberately selects that portion of the available evidence that supports his theory of communal sentiments or its new-fangled substitute 'community consciousness'. The 'theory in his head' takes precedence over historical materials. This is, if anything, a trifle peculiar from somebody who prefers to preach with E.P. Thompson's celebrated dictum as his guiding epigraph. Is it too much to expect that someone who goes on hectoring about 'how to write good history' should practice, at least, some of his own precepts?

I have argued that, in the 1870s and 1880s, faced with the uncongenial world in the towns and industries of colonial capitalism, the pioneer workers responded with 'strike-in-detail'. This behaviour was provoked not by a desire to change their working conditions or wages but to maintain their pre-industrial work behaviour, as far as possible. In the 1890s, however, there was a new state of ferment among the jute mill workers that found manifestation in a heightening of group and, at times, mass action. Several cases of collective action—deputations, disorders, strikes, violent troubles, riots, and so on—occurred. To reiterate my position, they did not express a clarified sociopolitical goal or comprehend the basic antagonism involved, but these protests do show that the workers were trying to improve their lot through collective action. The crucial difference in the 1890s was the nature of the grievances: wages, length of the working day, oppression of sardars, festival holidays, and other industrial matters. These incidents, however represented only the tip of an iceberg—the existence of widespread dissatisfaction among not only the jute mill workers but among the labouring poor of Calcutta. It is this dissatisfaction that found a dramatic expression in the Talla riot.

Chakrabarty is, however, determined to ignore the significance of all this. For him, demands like festival holidays can only have a community-centric implication. But in my view, the context was more complex and this must not be glossed over. These have been elaborated and analysed in my Occasional Paper (pp. 134–8). My point is that in the conditions prevailing in those days, the emerging working class was desperately short of means of resistance to the new ways of exploitation and authority and had to resort to everything including religion.

Chakrabarty takes exception to my characterization of the term 'community consciousness' as being 'too narrow'. But this characterization was made in the course of discussing the demand for festival holidays (Occasional Paper 22, p. 137). I made the further observation, 'In view of all these we should be chary in making generalization about community consciousness. The demand for religious festival holidays certainly indicated a community-feeling. But it was mingled with something broader than this' (Occasional Paper 22, p. 141). Chakrabarty does not agree with this reasoning and rejects it. He does not give any reason or argument. He merely asserts (a) that Das Gupta 'does not stop to think how the specific cultural past of jute workers relates to the questions of class consciousness' and (b) that Das Gupta draws 'a quite superficial and unwarranted' parallel with the history of the English working class (Critique, p. 11).

This really is not a sufficient reason to reject my argument. Even if I grant for argument's sake that the parallel drawn is wrong, but what does that have to do with my main line of argument and interpretation in relation to jute workers' demand for festival holidays? Also, is the parallel drawn so unjustified, as Chakrabarty tries to make it out? He refers to various authorities to establish his point: E.J. Hobsbawm is one of them. But it is Hobsbawm who with reference to Dissenting Labour Sects speaks of 'proletarian organizations and aspirations of a sort expressed through traditional religious ideology'.[4] Again, 'it was .... natural for the common people to use religious language to express their first aspirations....'[5] Sure enough, there are very important differences between dissenting Christianity in Britain and Islam or Hinduism in Bengal. But no mechanical parallel has been drawn; the differences in the two situations have been hinted at in my paper (Occasional Paper 22, pp. 135–8).

So far as (a) is concerned, the accusation made against me is quite unfair. For in dealing with the demand for holidays on the occasion of festivals, I have been exactly trying to do what I am accused of not doing. Throughout I have tried to understand, examine, and explain the influence of the cultural past in the lives of the first-generation jute mill workers. I, of course, have not considered the influence of the cultural past in its entirety. My focus has been on one particular but important aspect, that is, religion. I have tried to show how the forms of traditional religion, which had encompassed the lives of common people for centuries, affected the early industrial workers (Occasional Paper 22, pp. 95–100, 134–8).

Chakrabarty's several other specific criticisms of my paper warrant some comments. He rejects the concluding observations I made. In his presentation of my view, I am supposed to have spoken of class consciousness of the jute workers in the 1890s (Critique, pp. 2, 7).

Further, I am represented by him as arguing that 'the working class anywhere is born with an instinct for moving towards class consciousness' (p. 8). May I submit that Chakrabarty actually makes a caricature of my analysis? While he professes 'to quote Das Gupta in extenso on class consciousness' (p. 7), he in practice omits significant portions and mutilates my argument.

So let me quote the relevant portions from the section entitled 'Towards Working Class Forms of Action and Class Feeling':

It may be stated that the workers in the 1890s ... increasingly resorted to characteristically working class forms of action—combinations, active interventions and direct group actions .... It is tempting to belittle the significance of these actions ... But what deserves emphasis is that in their demands, and also in their way of action, a striving of the workers, no doubt in an obscure and muddled fashion, towards going beyond their immediate situation was clearly discernible.... Thus, here was the birth of a *class-feeling*—a feeling of an identity of interests as between the workers themselves and as against the employers... It was *not yet class-consciousness—neither political consciousness nor even the trade union consciousness* which Lenin was speaking of, for St. Petersburg in this period [emphasis added]. Yet it was an *advance* from the narrow level of social feeling of not only the peasantry, but also of the broader mass of urban poor. And in defending as well advancing its immediate interests, the *transitional* work force was trying, of course in a rambling and sporadic fashion [emphasis added], to overcome its part-human, depersonalized, disembodied condition of existence, to establish working class and human rights and to get on the road towards self-awareness and working class consciousness.[6]

It is possible to agree or disagree with the above passage. But by no stretch of rarefied imagination can it be derived that I have described the workers in the 1890s as exhibiting class consciousness. If Chakrabarty had read the piece with a modicum of humility and attention, he would have noted that I was making a very cautious and qualified statement. In fact, here a clear distinction was being made between three categories: class feeling, trade union consciousness, and class consciousness. And such a distinction is present in Marxist analysis. 'Class feeling' encompasses something more than what Chakrabarty thinks ('hatred and hostility' for the rich, Critique, p. 13). This is clearly indicated by the fact that specific demands were formulated by the workers in the 1890s, and the obvious aims of these were limited reform of the prevailing state of affairs. I have viewed all this as class feeling as the workers were going beyond isolated and individual feeling and reaction found in the 1870s and 1880s and resorting to group and collective, that is, social expression of their resentment and aspirations.[7]

Chakrabarty asks the question: 'If the workers *felt* an identity of interests between themselves and against their employers, weren't they, for all practical purposes, class conscious...?' (Critique, p. 13; emphasis in original). This seems to be a strangely muddled notion of class consciousness and more than a little surprising when it comes from someone who gives the impression of being familiar with classical Marxism and its more sophisticated twentieth-century variants.

In Marx's terms, proletarian class consciousness involves not merely a sense or feeling but a pervasive understanding and comprehension of the proletariat's position and role in the economy and society; it also involves an intellectual or theoretical articulation of that understanding, and also a conscious and active striving for bringing about a revolutionary transformation of the economy and society through a formal organization including mediation of a political organization.[8] In this context, the jute mill workers in the 1890s manifested just class feeling, at which they had arrived at instinctively or, what in my view is the same thing, spontaneously.

Chakrabarty, however, strongly, objects to the use of the term 'instinctive'. He attributes to me 'an "instinctive" view of class consciousness'. Marx, Engels, and Lenin, the founding fathers of Marxist theory and practice, have themselves spoken of 'the instinct of rebellion' against capitalist exploitation. Their writings clearly suggest spontaneous generation of discontent as well as certain aspirations as distinct from 'class consciousness' from the objective position of the proletariat.[9]

My observation that 'the workers in the 1890s were haltingly discovering .... certain elementary rules and truth about class warfare' is also found to be objectionable by Chakrabarty. Ridiculing this, he writes, 'Indeed, his [Das Gupta's] .... workers '*discover* [emphasis Chakrabarty's] ... rules and truth of class warfare—rules and truths that were already obviously there—by the very fact of being workers, so great is their "epistemological privilege"' (Critique, p. 8). In his zeal to ridicule, he misses the main point. The position is not whether any rule is laid down somewhere waiting to be discovered. It is an essential aspect of social reality that the workers, and indeed any subordinate group or class, because of their position in class society, cannot make things move unless they act collectively. The jute workers in their first generation of existence were discovering this truth through their experience of labour and life. Chakrabarty, however, is oblivious of all this.

For Chakrabarty, historical processes are to be seen in black or white; shades of grey are irrelevant. Hence, there can either be community consciousness or class consciousness. A work force cannot exhibit, for Chakrabarty, the multiplex reality of overlapping levels of interests, feelings, and consciousness. Thus, workers must show either an 'indifference to work' or a 'willingness to work' (Critique, p. 12); an organization must be pro-Muslim, anti-Hindu, or an anti-British labour organization. (See Chakrabarty's treatment of the Mahomedan Association.) Change or flux or process of formation are to be glossed over. History, unfortunately, is not so neat, and complexities relating to change or process are of some relevance to a serious study of labour history.

Notes and References

1. 'Critique' here refers to 'Class Consciousness and Labour History of Bengal: A Critique of Ranajit Das Gupta's Paper "Material Conditions and Behavioural Aspects of Calcutta Working Class 1875–99"'.

2. Repeatedly, he states that his almost only concern in the paper is with the 'communal culture' of jute mill workers (CRL, p. 1), 'the history of communal violence in the city', 'the beginnings of the tradition of "politics of mass communal violence" in Calcutta' (CRL, p. 2), those demands 'of the immigrant mill hands and the city poor' 'that essentially represented community issues, and that at times bordered on communalism' (CRL, p. 9), 'a growing communal culture' (CRL, p. 11), and rioting by mill hands on 'communal issues' (CRL, p. 19). In the same vein, he writes that 'communal sentiments were not confined to the jute mill labourers only, they seem to have been shared in the very same period by certain other groups of the city's labouring poor too'. Continuing, he states, 'These men participated in some

communal riots that broke out in Calcutta and in the suburbs in the 1890s' (CRL, p. 2).

3. See Parliamentary Papers, 1909, vol. 63, Indian Factory Labour Commission 1908, evidence, witness no. 63.

4. E.J. Hobsbawm, *Social Bandits and Primitive Rebels* (Manchester: Manchester University Press, 1959), 7.

5. Hobsbawm, *Social Bandits and Primitive Rebels*, 145; see also 126–7, 129–30.

6. Das Gupta, 'Material Conditions and Behavioural Aspects of Calcutta Working Class 1875–1899,' 150–1; if not stated otherwise, emphasis in the original.

7. Chakrabarty is factually wrong when he asserts that 'there was not even a single strike in which all the workers of a mill combined' (Critique, p. 7). In fact, at least three instances of mill-wise strikes and group actions—Kankinara Jute Mill and Budge Budge Jute Mill strikes of 1895 and Baranagore Jute Mill strike of 1896—have been mentioned in my paper (pp. 89–92).

8. See Karl Marx, *The Poverty of Philosophy* (Moscow: Progress Publishers, 1955), 192–5; and Karl Marx and Frederick Engels, 'Manifesto of the Communist Party' in *Selected Works*, vol. I (Moscow, 1950), 40–1, 42.

9. See Marx, *The Poverty of Philosophy*, 192–5; Marx and Engels, 'Manifesto of the Communist Party,' 40–1, and F. Engels, *The Conditions*

of the Working Class in England (Moscow: Progress Publisher, 1973), 255–6, 261–2. Lenin used the very term 'instinct' in the sense of 'unconsciousness (spontaneity)' in the context of generation of trade union consciousness. Thus, he writes, 'instinct is that unconsciousness (spontaneity) [giving rise to trade union consciousness] to the aid of which Socialists must come' (V.I. Lenin, 'What Is to Be Done', *Collected Works*, Vol. 5, 368).

Index